The Singers

A play based on the folktale *The Bremen Town Musicians*

Retold by Pauline Cartwright
Illustrated by Fiona Lee

Contents

NARRATOR

DONKEY

DOG

ROOSTER

CAT

ROBBER 1

ROBBER 2

ROBBER 3

ROBBER 4

Act 1:
The Roadside

NARRATOR Once there was a donkey walking along the road.

DONKEY *Hee-haw!* I have to leave my home because my owner thinks I'm old. He won't feed me as much as he used to, because I can't carry as much as I used to. I can't help getting old. *Hee-haw! Hee-haw!* So I've run away.

NARRATOR As the donkey walked along, he met a dog sitting on the roadside.

DONKEY What are you doing sitting by the road?

DOG *Woof-woof!* I'm homeless. I've been thrown out because my owner thinks I am too slow. What shall I do? Where shall I go?

NARRATOR The sad dog began to howl loudly.

DOG *Oooooowwww! Oooooowwww! Ooooooowwwwww!*

DONKEY I've run away from my home. I'm going to Bremen town to become a singer. *Hee-haw! Hee-haw!* I have a very fine voice, like you have. Come with me to Bremen town and we can become singers together.

DOG What a marvellous idea! *Woof! Woof! Woof-woof!*

NARRATOR So the dog got up and walked off down the road with the donkey. In a little while, they met a cat.

DONKEY *Hee-haw!* You're looking very sad, Cat. My friend Dog was looking sad before, but now she's happy again. Why are you sad?

CAT My owner sent me away because I don't hunt mice any more. I'm old. *Meow! Meow!*

DONKEY Then you must come with us and be a singer! We're off to Bremen town. You sing very well. Come with us, and we can sing as we go.

NARRATOR So off went the donkey, the dog and the cat, all singing together. Then they came upon a rooster.

DOG *Woof! Woof!* Hello, Rooster. Are you well?

ROOSTER I'm not at all well. *Cock-a-doodle-do!* How can I enjoy life without a farm to live on?

DONKEY *Hee-haw!* What has happened to your farm, Rooster?

ROOSTER I've had to run away. My owner wanted to cook me for lunch! *Cock-a-doodle-doo! Doodle-doo!* Now I don't know where I should go.

DONKEY Well, you must come with us. You have a very fine voice. We're off to Bremen town to sing.

DOG You can sing with us. *Woof! Woof!*

NARRATOR So the rooster went with the donkey, the dog and the cat. Off they went braying and crowing, yowling and howling. They looked for a place to stay for the night.

Act 2: The House

CAT Hush now. I see a house around this corner. *Meow!* There's smoke coming out of the chimney. I would so love to sit by a fire. *Meow! Meow!*

DONKEY *Hee-haw!* I'll go and peep in the window. I'll see if there's anyone there who might let us come in.

DOG Stretch up high, Donkey. That's it. Now what do you see? *Woof-woof!* What do you see?

DONKEY *Hee-haw! Hee-haw!* Robbers! Robbers in this house! They are feasting on the best dinner I've ever seen. It looks really, really delicious.

CAT If only it was us in there eating such a fine feast. *Meow! Meow!*

ROOSTER I wish it was us, too. I'm very hungry. *Cock-a-doodle-doo!* We need a plan to get those robbers out. Then we can eat at that table.

DONKEY You're right, Rooster. *Hee-haw!* Let's make a plan.

NARRATOR So the animals talked together and made a plan. This is what they did. The dog stood on the donkey's back, the cat stood on the dog's back, and the rooster stood on the cat's head. They could all see in the window.

DONKEY Begin!

NARRATOR Together, they began braying and crowing, yowling and howling. The robbers jumped up in fright.

ROBBER 1 A fearsome monster is trying to come in!

ROBBER 2 I can see the terrible shape of it!

ROBBER 3 It's going to come through the window!

ROBBER 4 Quick! Quick! We must go before it comes in and gets us all!

NARRATOR The robbers ran out of the house. The animals stopped singing and laughed.

ROOSTER *Cock-a-doodle-doo! Doodle-doo!* It was a very good plan. The robbers have gone!

CAT Good! *Meow*! We can eat all the dinner we want now.

DONKEY Follow me, my friends. *Hee-haw!*

NARRATOR The animals went inside the house and sat around the table.

DOG *Woof-woof!* How delicious! Dear friends, how wonderful to be here with you all.

ROOSTER *Doodle-doo!* I am so hungry.

DONKEY There's plenty for all of us. What a scrumptious feast! *Hee-haw! Hee-haw!*

CAT And a fire to sleep beside as well. *Purrrrrrr.*

NARRATOR The animals ate until they could eat no more. Then they put new logs on the fire and found comfortable sleeping places.

DONKEY I do like a soft bed. *Hee-haw! Snore-snore-snore.*

NARRATOR The donkey stretched out on the couch and fell fast asleep.

DOG I like to be off the floor, too, and somewhere soft.

NARRATOR The dog scrambled into an armchair and went to sleep.

CAT *Meow!* By the fire for me! *Purrrrr. Purrrrrr.*

NARRATOR The cat curled up on the mat and went to sleep.

ROOSTER *Cock-a-doodle-doo! Doodle-doodle-doo!*

NARRATOR The rooster climbed high up on a beam in the ceiling and fell sound asleep.

Act 4: Good Music

NARRATOR At midnight, the robbers came back to check if the fearsome animal had gone away.

ROBBER 1 It's very quiet. Maybe the terrible monster didn't go into the house after all.

ROBBER 2 Shall we go in and see? I didn't try that wonderful cake.

ROBBER 3 Cake. I could eat some cake, especially with some of that ice-cream.

ROBBER 4 I don't like walking about in the night. What I'd like is a good sleep.

NARRATOR The cat heard the robbers talking and opened one eye. She sat up and whispered to the others.

CAT *Meow!* I think it's time to sing again. The robbers are back!

NARRATOR The robbers crept through the door. The animals waited quietly in their sleeping places.

ROBBER 1 I'm sure there is no-one here. It's very quiet.

ROBBER 2 I just hope the ice-cream hasn't melted. I do like ice-cream with cake.

ROBBER 3 I can still see the fire going. That means the ice-cream will have melted.

ROBBER 4 Oh, come on. The rest of the food will be fine. Stop talking and let's start eating!

DONKEY *Hee-haw!* Begin!

NARRATOR Together, the animals began braying and crowing, howling and yowling.

ROBBER 1 Oh no! It's here! The terrible monster is here!

ROBBER 2 Quickly! Run!

NARRATOR The robbers tripped over each other, trying to get out of the house.

ROOSTER *Cock-a-doodle-doodle-doo! Doodle-doodle-doo!*

ROBBER 3 Ooooh! What a terrible cry!

ROBBER 4 Run, everybody! Run!

NARRATOR The robbers ran for their lives, far away into the woods.

DONKEY *Hee-haw! Hee-haw!* Some people just don't like good music.

DOG No, they don't. *Woof-woof*! And I'm very glad.

CAT *Meow!* So am I. Now I can get back to sleep.

ROOSTER *Cock-a-doodle-doo!* I'll wake you all when it's morning.

NARRATOR The animals knew the robbers would not be back. They ate a small snack and smiled a lot. Then they settled down in their comfortable places to sleep.

In the morning, they decided they wouldn't bother going to Bremen town after all. They would stay right here, four happy singers in a lovely home.

DONKEY *Hee-haw!*

DOG *Woof-woof!*

CAT *Meow!*

ROOSTER *Cock-a-doodle-do!*